Bert's Little Secret

Written by RM Morrissey

Illustrated by Ila Taylor Bologni

First Published 2021 by RMorrissey Books

ISBN: 9798532257252

Copyright © RM Morrissey, 2021

The right of RM Morrissey to be identified as the author of this work has been asserted in accordance with the Copyright, Designs and Patents Act, 1988.

All rights reserved. No part of this publication may be reproduced, stored in a retrieval system, or transmitted, in any form or by any means (electronic, mechanical, photocopying, recording or otherwise), without the prior written permission of the publisher.

A CIP catalogue record for this book is available from the British Library.

For links to free content and to be updated on future book releases, follow me on Instagram

@rmorrisseybooks

Bert the Caterpillar had been feeling kind of down for a very long time. For as far back as he could remember, he couldn't think of a moment when he wasn't worried. He didn't know what to do with this worry, or how to tell others about it, so he just kept it inside.

It became his little secret.

Day after day, Bert decided that today was the day he would get up and do something. But instead, he just grabbed a mouthful of leaves from out the window and snuggled back into his bed, sighing to himself,
"Maybe tomorrow."

All of Bert's friends were worried about him because they didn't like it when their friends were sad. They tried to cheer him up with the things they thought he would like.

Bali the Bumblebee brought Bert a basket of fresh bluebell flowers. Bert's favourite breakfast! Bali was sure he saw a smile crack across Bert's face when he said thanks.

But when Bali asked Bert if he wanted to go play hopscotch, all he got in reply was as a sigh, "Maybe tomorrow."

A little while later, Layla the Ladybird visited Bert too! She brought a bag brimming with four-leaf clovers. Bert's favourite lunch! And just like Bali, she saw a smile crack across Bert's face when he said thanks.

But when Layla asked Bert if he wanted to go play tag, all she got in reply was a sigh, "Maybe tomorrow."

That night, Philip the Firefly came knocking at Bert's door. He brought Bert a delicious bunch of apple blossoms. Bert's favourite dinner! Philip was sure that he saw a smile crack across Bert's face when he said thanks.

But when Philip asked Bert if he wanted to go play jump rope, all he got in reply was a sigh, "Maybe tomorrow."

Day after day, Bert's friends brought him things he liked to eat and Bert was thankful but it didn't make him feel any better.

Inside, Bert felt different, like something was wrong. He felt like he was different on the inside, but he couldn't explain it and didn't know how to tell his friends about his worry.

And his friends didn't ask, so he just kept it inside.
His little secret.

Bert didn't know why, but one day he wanted to go for a walk. So he got up out of bed, had a quick mouthful of leaves for breakfast and left his home before he ended up back in bed, under his covers, like every other day.

Bert passed Bali playing hopscotch with the other bumblebees, but he got scared when Bali asked him if he wanted to play and nervously said, "Ah - umm - maybe tomorrow."

As Bert went on, he passed Layla playing tag with the other ladybirds, but he got scared when Layla asked him if he wanted to play and nervously said, "Ah - umm - maybe tomorrow."

A little further on, Bert passed Philip jumping rope with the other fireflies, but he got scared when Philip asked him if he wanted to play and nervously said, "Ah - umm - maybe tomorrow."

Bert came to his favourite tree and climbed up to his favourite branch to sit and think. He wanted to tell his friends, but he didn't know the right way to do it.

Part of Bert felt happy inside that all his friends kept asking him to play with them even though he kept telling them tomorrow. But part of Bert still ached because he had that worry inside. A feeling that something was different, something that he couldn't explain.

It worried him that who his friends thought he was, wasn't really him. What if they didn't like him for who he truly was?

As Bert was thinking, Alice the Ant came crawling by.

"Hi Bert!" she said. "Can I sit with you?"

Bert replied, "Maybe tomorrow."

"Bert, that doesn't make any sense," Alice laughed.

Bert laughed too.
"No, it doesn't make sense, does it? Yes, you can sit with me."

"Alice, can I tell you something?"

"Sure thing, Bert."

Bert explained to Alice how he felt different inside, like he was something else. Something that his friends didn't know he truly was. Alice just sat there listening to him. She didn't interrupt, she just let him speak.

Bert cried a little when he told her that he was worried his friends wouldn't want to be his friend if he changed who he was. He cried and he got out all of his worries. Alice just sat there with an arm around his shoulder, listening like a good friend.

When he was done, Alice hugged her friend close and told him gently, "Bert, you're my friend no matter what. If you woke up tomorrow as a girl, you'd still be my friend. If you couldn't walk anymore, I'd help you get to where you needed to be. If your skin changed to be a rainbow of colours, you can still call me your friend."

Bert sniffled a little. And he felt the weight inside him shrink. His worries started to seem a bit silly with his friend talking to him. He began to open his mouth to speak ...

"I'm not done yet, Bert! You're my friend no matter what and it doesn't matter who or what you are on the inside. Real friends stick together, even when things are difficult or scary. I'm really glad you shared your worries with me Bert. Thank you for being my friend."

Bert hugged his friend Alice. "Thank you for being my friend too."

Bert walked home feeling more free than he had ever felt before. For as far back as he could remember, he couldn't think of a moment when he felt this good about who he was on the inside and out. He shared his worry with a good friend and she loved him all the same.

Bert was ready to show others who he really was inside.
It could no longer be his little secret.

At home, Bert didn't climb into his bed like he usually did, but instead hung from his ceiling and spun himself a soft and warm silk cocoon. He closed his eyes and said good night, ready to show his friends who he was inside.

A beautiful butterfly.

ACKNOWLEDGMENTS

Thank you to all of the children who have given me excellent feedback on the many, many many versions of this book. It has been a wonderful experience working with you, listening to your likes and dislikes.

Children truly make excellent editors!

If you enjoyed reading the book, consider following me on Instagram for links to free content and to be updated on future book releases.

@rmorrisseybooks

Want More?

Download a FREE ebook written by RM Morrissey

https://linktr.ee/rmorrisseybooks

Printed in Great Britain
by Amazon